What Do You Know?

A Catholic Identity Game
for the Whole Community

What Do YOU Know?

PEGGY O'NEILL FISHER

A Catholic
Identity Game
for the Whole
Community

TWENTY
THIRD *23rd*
PUBLICATIONS

Dedication

To my family, Edward, Nancy, Pete, and Tom,
to Mary Jane and Harold who encouraged and nurtured us,
and to all the families who have helped us grow in our faith.

Twenty-Third Publications
A Division of Bayard
One Montauk Avenue, Suite 200
New London, CT 06320
(860) 437-3012 or (800) 321-0411
www.23rdpublications.com

ISBN 978-1-58595-586-2
Library of Congress Catalog Card Number: 2006920450
Printed in the U.S.A.

Contents

Introduction

We meet our God in time and space. These encounters are sacred in our memory, and we take time to name and reverence them. For this reason we have a liturgical year filled with celebrations of feast and season. We remember and bring into our present lives those mysteries of our God and heroic deeds of our saints that inspire us in our lives as Catholic Christians.

Whole community catechesis offers us a wonderful opportunity to share our faith and our religious heritage in a multigenerational setting. Here we learn from each other and engage in activities that enhance both our catholic literacy and our practice of the faith.

Catholic Literacy

cath•o•lic (**kath**-lik) adj: of or relating to or supporting Catholicism; "the Catholic Church"

lit•er•a•cy (**lit**-er-*uh*-see) n: the condition or quality of being knowledgeable in a particular subject or field

Catholic literacy requires familiarity with the terms and concepts that we, as members of the Catholic Christian community, use to name what we do and who we are. Such familiarity is not a measure of our faith, holiness, or practice of charity. Catholic literacy, rather, is a partner of good catechesis and lively worship within a vibrant, serving community.

I grew up in the pre-Vatican II Church, learning Latin phrases and the correct words for all things related to the Church. I knew the Church's process for proclaiming saints and electing a pope. The fruits and gifts of the Holy Spirit, as well as the rules regarding fasting during Lent, were also part of my Catholic literacy.

Then the Second Vatican Council seemed to set the Church on end. We experienced the loss of a certain Catholic literacy as the Church changed and updated. As the years passed, much of the rich meaning of our liturgy, Church environment, and practices were lost to the next generation.

In an attempt to pass on our Catholic identity to my own children, I created games based on the seasons. I cut out cards with questions printed on them and left them out in obvious places. Sure enough, we would end up going through the questions and discussing the answers. As the years went by, we used these games with other families, confirmation peer groups, and the families in our local faith formation program. The games prompted rich discussion and much laughter.

For the past dozen years, our small parish community has used a family model of faith formation. We started even when there weren't curriculum materials or learning aids available for our intergenerational model. During those first meetings we gathered around a table, eating donuts and trying to get parents and children talking together. Then I shared one of the games created for my family. At one of our first fall gatherings, we used the Angels set. From that game we moved into a discussion of the arrival of darkness and winter, the care God continually shows us, and the prayers that are part of our Catholic tradition.

Over the years we moved through the months with games about Advent, Epiphany, carnival, Lent, and Easter. Concerned that the families had used these games long enough, one month I left out the game. But participants asked questions such as, "Where's the game?" "Why don't we have questions at our table?" I found the games to be a consistent way for each family member to participate in our gatherings and to feel comfortable in the meeting space.

In our parish faith formation program we have now included more tables for participants, as well as better food! But the games continue, and Catholic literacy increases. Sometimes I scramble to create a new game or choose a game from last year, or a couple of years ago, and we use it again. The learners in the program grow and change. It's amazing what participants remember. This year one of our public school confirmation teens was delighted to know something her Catholic school peers did not. During many of our games she had rolled her eyes and acted disinterested, but she had actually learned more than she let on.

Without a certain level of Catholic literacy, we miss important aspects of our tradition. Without a familiarity with our Church environment we lose some of the symbolism that enriches our understanding of the liturgy. Without the correct terms we don't have the tools to discuss the deeper truths of our faith and ponder the connection between what happens in church and what happens in our everyday life. Catholic literacy is never an end in itself, but an aid in our process of growing, praying, and serving as Catholic Christians.

Whole Community Catechesis

whole (hohl) adj: 1. containing all components; complete; 2. not divided or disjoined; in one unit

com•mu•ni•ty (*kuh*-**myoo**-ni-tee) n: a group of people having ethnic or cultural or religious characteristics in common

cat•e•che•sis (kat-i-**kee**-sis) n: oral religious instruction (as before baptism or confirmation)

Early Christian communities did not have textbooks, curriculum consultants, online resources, or classrooms. Catechesis consisted of instruction by word of mouth, which involved a person-to-person offer of new life. Now we live in a society that has a well-developed educational system. We talk about magnet and charter schools, scholarships and grants, budgets and resources. Whole community catechesis doesn't need a variety of educational accoutrements but rather, faithful Christians. We echo the word to one another in the stories we tell and the adventures we share with members of our community, young and old.

Probably the hardest thing to adjust to in a whole community gathering is that it is not a classroom setting, even though we sometimes meet in rooms that are, look like, and/or feel like classrooms. In intergenerational settings we naturally adjust to all levels of ability and participation. Discussions more closely follow the model of the family dinner table. Younger members are delighted to be included in the group and receive unqualified acceptance. We know from learning theory that we learn much better and with more lasting results when we are in a comfortable, affirming meeting space.

Sometimes we are asked what type of program we have available for learners with disabilities. When households join together to grow in their faith, everyone has a different level of learning. Parents are present to create the proper environment for their children, and other participants easily follow that lead. Only when there is a graded program do teachers and parents assume that a certain group of learners have similar abilities and needs.

In this age of mobile families, the extended Church community can become a very valuable partner to parents and families. For example, as our children grew, my husband and I were hours away from our extended families. In their place, we gradually gathered other families with whom we celebrate our faith. Our local "grandparents" were able to communicate reverence and awareness to our children. The annual Epiphany gathering included acting out the Scripture. Even as sophisticated high schoolers, our children took part in donning the bathrobes and portraying the scenes. The special relationship they had with their faith family allowed then to put aside embarrassment and enter into the living story.

We also have field trips in our faith community. Once a year we borrow a school bus and visit another local church or site of religious importance. Before boarding the bus we share a meal and some sort of literacy-building activity for all ages. A very valuable part of these adventures is the stories and memories that we hear from the older members of our group.

As part of our faith formation we visit our own worship space during our monthly gathering. We see and name articles that are specific to our faith. Even young learners have a chance to see the oils taken out of the ambry. They get to smell the chrism. They see what is in the tabernacle and learn why one day a year the sanctuary lamp is not lit. Each child drops one grain of incense on the hot coal and sees the incense rise. Adults have a chance to be amazed along with the young learners when these experiences involve an intergenerational group.

We meet our God in time and space. Catholic literacy requires knowing the terms and meanings for the time and space in which we as Catholics live our faith. Passing on that information within our community, from one member to another, is an important part of whole community catechesis. Again, Catholic literacy is not an end in itself but a tool to use on the journey that leads us to know, love, and serve our God.

The Games

Community style

Try using these games in your parish community with an intergenerational group:

- as an icebreaker at the table while people are gathering;
- to allow young learners as well as adults to be successful at answering the questions (a few "give-away" questions are always included for the children);
- to deliver some basic information (this is done on the answer sheet that is included);
- to prepare the group for the learning that will take place during the session;
- to review material after a presentation;
- to review with a sacramental preparation group.

In the domestic Church

These games work just as well in your own home with your family as they do in the parish setting. Following is a three-step method families can use with their children.

1. The set-up

Which one of us hasn't motivated our children to eat vegetables or found just the right incentive to get the table set? It's all in the approach. With these games, suspense has to be built. Parents can put out the cards before the appropriate day. For example, in the middle of June, place a shell-shaped dish on the table containing a set of sand-colored shells with questions about the birth of John the Baptizer (June 24). Leave the container in an obvious place without any explanation so that the children notice the set and begin to ask about the answers.

2. The moment

When curiosity is at its peak, children are ready to absorb information, and they have fun doing it. It is a temptation to give answers, but the families will only give hints and explain where to begin the search. A dictionary, an atlas, and a Bible are the best tools. Try using the cards together as a family. One evening after supper use a quiz-show format.

3. The real learning

This discussion naturally follows or interrupts the game along the way. Here we let the Spirit guide us. The real-life questions that follow the games come when we are playing chauffeur or listening to the experiences of each other's days. These are the true teaching moments in the domestic Church.

Preparation for the Game

1. Make a copy of the question sheet and answer sheet on matching paper or card stock.

2. Fold the answer sheet in half.

3. Cut apart the ten questions.

4. Store the answer folder and the ten question cards in a plastic zipper storage bag and write the topic on bag.

Instructions

1. Choose one person to be the answer keeper and give the folder to that person. Intermediate-grade learners love to be the answer keeper.

2. Deal out the ten cards to the other players.

3. The card holder with the first question reads the question and gives an answer or passes.

4. Others who think they know a better answer can raise their hand to be called on by the card holder.

5. The answer keeper now reads the answer to the first question exactly as it is written, even if the right answer has been given.

6. Repeat steps 3, 4, and 5 with the remaining cards in numerical sequence.

Notes: When a question asks for the meaning of a word, give the dictionary definition, not the Church definition, unless otherwise noted. The portion of the answer following a colon, comma, or dash is additional information.

Scoring

After each question, the answer keeper decides who answered the question correctly. That person keeps the question card. The person with the most cards at the end of the game is the winner.

Be sure to have the following resources available: the *New American Bible* with revised New Testament, a college dictionary, and a world atlas.

Throughout the games where CCC is used, it refers to the *Catechism of the Catholic Church*, which is available in both hardcover and paperback. This book is a very valuable resource for adults. Take some time after the games to look up the various references for more information and to help increase your knowledge of the faith. Just remember that the Catechism is written as a resource for writers and teachers, not as a textbook for your family.

Our Solar Calendar

Since the days of our ancestors who hunted and farmed, people have kept track of time using natural events, such as the rising and setting of the sun, the location of the sun in the sky, and the change of the seasons. As people began to farm, they knew by the seasons when to plant and when to harvest. Humans created the first crude calendars to keep track of time by placing marks on a stone or a stick. As millennia passed, people developed more sophisticated calendars. A calendar based on the sun's location in the sky is called a solar calendar.

In the Northern hemisphere we experience the longest day of the year near the end of June and the shortest day near the end of December. We call these days the summer solstice and the winter solstice. Halfway in between the solstices we observe days of equal daylight and darkness. These are the spring or vernal equinox and the fall or autumnal equinox. Between these four main markers of the solar year we have cross-quarter days at the beginning of May, August, November, and February.

For many centuries, people of different cultures have celebrated the changing seasons with feasts and festivals. When individuals became Christians, they continued to celebrate these seasonal occurrences but changed the focus of their celebrations to reflect their belief in the Son of God who became human.

We can find many helpful books and Web sites about our calendar and how it came to be. Search your library and the Internet for the history of the calendar. Look up terms like "ancient calendars," "solar calendar," "Celtic calendar," and "quarter days" for more information.

Christian Solar Feasts

Our Church year begins four Sundays before Christmas with the Advent season of preparation. Over the two millennia of Christianity, the length of this preparation has varied from only a few days to a forty-day preparation. Christmas wasn't the first Christian feast of the child Jesus. The Epiphany on January 6 was the original celebration of the Incarnation. We observe the Epiphany to celebrate the manifestation of God in Jesus Christ to all nations.

Christmas comes near the shortest day of the year. Just as Jesus brought light into the world, the sun begins to shine a little longer each day after Christmas until the feast of John the Baptizer (June 24). From that date the days become shorter little by little until Christmas. This reflects the Scripture passage where John speaks of Jesus, saying, "He must increase, but I must decrease" (John 3:30). (We use Baptizer instead of Baptist, which also refers to a specific religious denomination, e.g., Southern Baptist.)

Since the birth of Jesus is celebrated on December 25, the Annunciation is observed nine months before. So we celebrate the Annunciation, or Mary Day, on March 25, near the spring equinox.

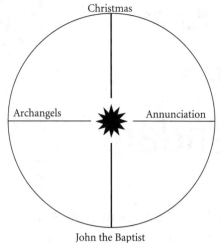

Christmas

Archangels

Annunciation

John the Baptist

The feast of the Archangels Michael, Gabriel, and Raphael is kept on September 29, near the fall equinox. Michael the Archangel protects us against darkness as the fall days become shorter and the time of darkness overcomes the daylight.

On the old Celtic calendar the New Year was celebrated on October 31, when the world seemed to be dying. Christians replaced the pagan revelry with their own remembrance of "those who have died and gone before us marked with the sign of faith." On November 1, we remember the saints, "since we are surrounded by so great a cloud of witnesses" (Hebrews 12:1). On All Souls Day (November 2) we remember all of our deceased sisters and brothers.

Detailed information about the solar calendar and Christian solar feasts can be found on the Internet or at the library. Search for "Halloween," "Catholic Christmas," "angels," and "Baptizer." You might also look for new ways to celebrate the solar-based holy days.

Solar Games

The Solar Calendar set of questions is a good way to introduce the rest of the game questions. The whole set easily matches the academic year, especially the fall and winter months.

Angels: September/October
All Saints and Saints: October/November
Advent: November/December
Christmas: December
Baptizer: December or June
Annunciation: December or March
Epiphany: January

Families can benefit from these games as well. They are great fun for a Christmas or Halloween party. A game might also fit for a family birthday party. In the summer, when there is time to observe the length of days, you can enjoy the Solar as well as the Baptizer and Christmas games.

A good introduction to Advent through the Baptism of the Lord is found in the book *Companion to the Calendar*, pages 2–11. This book also contains specific information about the Annunciation (March 25), the Birth of John the Baptist (June 23-24), and Halloween/All Saints Day/All Souls Day (October 31 and November 1-2).

A Child's First Catholic Dictionary contains terms and thoughtful illustrations that correlate with words found in each of the solar sets.

Solar: angel, Church Year, John the Baptist, Mary Mother of God, Son of God

Advent: Advent, Christmas, Emmanuel, Eucharist, Jesus the Christ, liturgical colors, Messiah, Word

Christmas: angel, Baptism of Jesus, Bethlehem, Church Year, Incarnation, Joseph, liturgical colors, manger, nativity

Epiphany: Christmas, Epiphany, gifts, gospel, Jew, wise men

Annunciation: angel, Annunciation, grace, Hail Mary, Mary Mother of God, Nazareth

The Baptizer: angel, Baptism, Baptism of Jesus, dove, forgiveness, Holy Spirit, John the Baptist, Messiah, Son of God

Angels: angel, Annunciation, evil, Hail Mary, John the Baptist, Mary Mother of God, Mass, prayer

All Saints: All Saints Day, All Souls Day, Baptism, communion of saints, death, heaven, holy, saint, everlasting life

Saints: Christian, creation, death, heaven, Joseph, martyr, Mary Mother of God, saint, Jesus the Christ, prayer, saint

Ordinary Time: Church Year, liturgical colors, Beatitudes

1. **Our Solar Calendar** QUESTION CARDS

1. What does the word **solar** relate to? 1	6. Whose birth do we celebrate near the summer solstice, the person who prepared the way of the Lord? 1
2. How long is a solar year? 1	7. Which day in the fall has equal daylight and darkness? 1
3. What do we call the shortest day of the year? 1	8. Which feast do we celebrate near the fall equinox to honor God's special messengers, like the one who came to Mary? 1
4. On which day near the winter solstice do we celebrate the birth of the Son of God? 1	9. What do we call the day in spring with equal sunlight and night? 1
5. What do we call the longest day of the year? 1	10. What celebration (near the spring equinox) recalls the angel asking Mary to be the mother of God? 1

1. **Our Solar Calendar** Answer Sheet

1. The sun

2. 364.25 days, the complete revolution of the earth around the sun

3. The winter solstice, which occurs on December 21 or 22

4. Christmas, celebrated on December 25

5. The summer solstice, which occurs on June 21 or 22

6. John the Baptizer, whose birth is celebrated on June 24

7. Autumnal or fall equinox, which occurs on September 22 or 23

8. The Feast of Michael, Gabriel, and Raphael, the Archangels, September 29

9. Vernal or spring equinox, which occurs on March 20 or 21

10. Annunciation, usually celebrated on March 25

2. **Advent** Question Cards

1. What special celebration do we prepare for during the Advent season? <div align="right">2</div>	6. What did the Hebrew people wait for throughout their history? <div align="right">2</div>
2. What does the word **Advent** mean? <div align="right">2</div>	7. When will Jesus come again in majesty? <div align="right">2</div>
3. Whose coming do we await during Advent? <div align="right">2</div>	8. What are some ways in which we experience the mystery of Jesus present today? <div align="right">2</div>
4. When does the Advent season begin? <div align="right">2</div>	9. What does the name **Emmanuel** mean? (Matthew 1:23) <div align="right">2</div>
5. What is the liturgical color for the season of Advent? <div align="right">2</div>	10. When does the Advent season end? <div align="right">2</div>

2. **Advent** Answer Sheet

1. Christmas, the birth of Jesus our savior

2. Arrival or coming

3. Jesus Christ

4. The Sunday closest to November 30, or the fourth Sunday before Christmas

5. Violet or blue-violet—some parishes use blue-violet to distinguish the Advent season of anticipation from the more penitential season of Lent

6. A savior or messiah (CCC #524, #1095)

7. At the end of time or of the world (CCC #681)

8. The many ways include the Eucharist shared; the word of God proclaimed; the assembly gathered; people who are in need, suffering, or oppressed (CCC #1373)

9. God with us

10. At sundown on Christmas Eve

3. **Christmas** Question Cards

1. Who are the mother and foster father of Jesus? (Luke 2:4–5)

    3

2. In what town was Jesus born? (Luke 2:4)

    3

3. What is a manger?

    3

4. What did the multitude of angels sing?

    3

5. Who were the first to visit the baby Jesus? (Luke 2:15–16)

    3

6. What do we call our celebration of the birth of Jesus?

    3

7. What is a Christmas crèche?

    3

8. What does the word **incarnation** tell us about Jesus?

    3

9. When does the Christmas season end?

    3

10. What is the liturgical color of the Christmas season?

    3

3. **Christmas** Answer Sheet

1. Mary and Joseph (CCC #437)

2. Bethlehem

3. A feed box for animals

4. "Glory to God in the highest and peace to God's people on earth."

5. The shepherds (CCC #525)

6. Christmas

7. A representation of Christ's nativity in the stable at Bethlehem, usually with statues or figurines

8. Jesus is truly God and truly human (CCC #464). The Latin word **carne** means flesh.

9. With the celebration of the Baptism of the Lord

10. White or sometimes gold

4. **Epiphany** Question Cards

1. Which gospel tells of the magi? 4	6. How did the wise ones learn not to return to Herod? (Matthew 2:12) 4
2. What did the wise men observe and follow? (Matthew 2:2) 4	7. How many magi or kings are there in your nativity set? 4
3. What news troubled Herod? (Matthew 2:3) 4	8. What does the word **Epiphany** mean? 4
4. Where did the magi find the child? (Matthew 2:11, Luke 2:7) 4	9. Which Shakespearean play is placed in the time setting of the Epiphany? 4
5. What gifts did the magi bring? (Matthew 2:11) 4	10. When do we celebrate the Epiphany in the United States? 4

4. **Epiphany** Answer Sheet

1. The Gospel of Matthew. The magi are sometimes called wise men, astrologers, or kings.

2. A star at its rising

3. That there was a newborn king of the Jews

4. In a house. Matthew speaks of a house while Luke says the child was laid in a manger.

5. Gold, frankincense, and myrrh. Read the verses of the carol "We Three Kings" to understand one meaning given to these gifts.

6. In a dream

7. Three is the usual number. Scripture does not tell us the number of magi. Since the gospel account speaks of three gifts, tradition tells us there were three magi.

8. Showing forth, manifestation, or revelation (CCC #528)

9. **Twelfth Night**—count the nights from Christmas until the eve of January 6, the traditional day of Epiphany.

10. The Sunday between January 2 and 8.

5. **Annunciation** Question Cards

1. Which angel appeared to Mary? (Luke 1:26)

    5

2. In what town and district did Mary live? (Luke 1:26)

    5

3. What did the angel Gabriel say to greet Mary?

    5

4. What does the word **hail** mean?

    5

5. What do we call God's life in us?

    5

6. Who was the kinswoman that Mary went to visit? (Luke 1:36)

    5

7. With what words did Elizabeth greet Mary? (Luke 1:42)

    5

8. What does the word **blessed** mean?

    5

9. What prayer contains the words of Gabriel and Elizabeth?

    5

10. What prayer is traditionally said three times during the day with the ringing of church bells?

    5

5. **Annunciation** Answer Sheet

1. Gabriel

2. The town of Nazareth in Galilee (CCC #488)

3. "Hail Mary, full of grace. The Lord is with you."

4. An enthusiastic or joyful greeting

5. Grace (CCC #1999)

6. Elizabeth, Mary's cousin

7. "Blessed are you among women, and blessed is the fruit of your womb."

8. Highly favored, worthy of honor

9. The Hail Mary or **Ave Maria**

10. The Angelus

6. **The Baptizer** Question Cards

1. Who were the parents of John the Baptizer? (Luke 1:5) 6	6. In what river was John baptizing? (Matthew 3:13, John 1:28) 6
2. With what words did the angel greet the frightened Zechariah? (Luke 1:13) 6	7. What message was John preaching? (Matthew 3:2, Luke 3:3) 6
3. On what date do we celebrate the birth of John the Baptizer? 6	8. Was John the Baptizer the Messiah? (Luke 3:15–16) 6
4. What did John the Baptizer wear when he was preaching in the desert? (Matthew 3:4, Mark 1:6) 6	9. After John baptized Jesus, who appeared in the form of a dove? (Matthew 3:16, Mark 1:10, Luke 4:21) 6
5. What did John the Baptizer eat? (Matthew 3:4, Mark 1:6) 6	10. What did the voice from heaven say about Jesus? (Matthew 3:17, Mark 1:11, Luke 3:22) 6

6. **The Baptizer** Answer Sheet

1. Zechariah and Elizabeth

2. "Do not be afraid."

3. On June 24, when the hours of sunlight begin to decrease. Just as John said about Jesus, "He must increase, I must decrease." (John 3:30)

4. Camel hair and a leather belt

5. Locusts and wild honey

6. Jordan River

7. The baptism of repentance for the forgiveness of sins (CCC #535)

8. No. John said, "The one who is coming is mightier than I."

9. The Holy Spirit (CCC #701)

10. "This is my Son, the Beloved."

7. **Angels** Question Cards

1. What does the word **angel** mean?

    7

2. On what date does the Church honor the angels Michael, Raphael, and Gabriel?

    7

3. Which angel do we ask to protect us against evil?

    7

4. Which angel announced that John the Baptizer would be born? (Luke 1:19)

    7

5. What did the angel Gabriel announce to Mary?

    (Luke 1:26–31)

    7

6. When do we celebrate the feast of the guardian angels?

    7

7. What prayer do we pray to our guardian angel?

    7

8. What song did the angels sing to praise God when Jesus was born?

    7

9. At Mass what do we sing "with all the choirs of angels…in their unending hymn of praise"?

    7

10. What United States city is sometimes called the "City of Angels"?

    7

7. **Angels** Answer Sheet

1. Messenger of God

2. On September 29, the feast of Michael, Gabriel, and Raphael, the Archangels

3. Michael the Archangel

4. Gabriel

5. That she would be the mother of Jesus

6. On October 2 (CCC #336)

7. Angel of God, my guardian dear, to whom God's love commits me here. Ever this day be at my side to light and guard, to rule and guide. Amen.

8. "Glory to God in the highest and peace to God's people on earth."

9. Holy, holy, holy, Lord God of power and might, heaven and earth are full of your glory. Hosanna in the highest.

10. Los Angeles: the full name is **El Pueblo de Nuestra Señora de los Angeles**, or the "City of Our Lady of the Angels"

8. **All Saints** Question Cards

1. When does the eve or vigil of a feast begin?

    8

2. What celebration was originally called All Hallows Eve?

    8

3. Halloween is the eve of what feast?

    8

4. What did the earliest Christians call all the baptized? (Romans 16:1–2; 1 Corinthians 16:1)

    8

5. What does the word **saint** mean?

    8

6. What day is chosen for a saint's feast days?

    8

7. What is the union of all Christians living and dead called?

    8

8. What do we celebrate on November 2?

    8

9. Whom do we remember and pray for on All Souls Day?

    8

10. In the Mexican tradition, what is the day called when the people remember and celebrate their departed?

    8

8. **All Saints** Answer Sheet

1. At sunset the night before the feast

2. Halloween

3. All Saints Day, when we celebrate the holiness of all saints known and unknown

4. Saints

5. A holy person who has died and gone to heaven

6. The date of their death, their birth into eternal life

7. The Communion of Saints, which includes the pilgrims on earth, the dead who are being purified, and the saints in glory (CCC #954)

8. All Souls Day

9. All who have died and who have not been proclaimed saints. Traditionally, we remember and pray for those who have died during the whole month of November.

10. **Dia de los Muertos**, or Day of the Dead

9. **Saints** Question Cards

1. What do we call a follower of Jesus who has lived a holy life, died, and gone to heaven?

   9

2. What do we call those who are put to death for their witness to Jesus Christ?

   9

3. What is the official process used by the Catholic Church to declare a person to be a saint?

   9

4. Which prayer is a series of saints' names with the petition "Pray for us" after each name?

5. Which saint is the foster father of Jesus?

   9

6. What is the name of the young woman who said "yes" and became the mother of Jesus?

   9

7. Which saint cut his cloak and gave half of it to a beggar suffering from the cold?

   9

8. Which female saint heard voices that told her to lead the army of France to save her country?

   9

9. Which saint loved and cared for all of God's creatures?

   9

10. Which saint was the first person Jesus appeared to after he rose from the dead?
    (Mark 16:9, John 20:11–18)

    9

9. **Saints** Answer Sheet

1. A saint

2. Martyrs, from the Greek word for witness (CCC #2473)

3. Canonization, a process begun in the tenth century. Before that, persons were declared saints by local communities after their death. (CCC #828)

4. The Litany of Saints

5. Joseph

6. Mary

7. Martin of Tours

8. Joan of Arc

9. Francis of Assisi

10. Mary Magdalene

10. **Ordinary Time** Question Cards

1. What are the first three cardinal numbers? 10	6. How many weeks are there in Ordinary Time? 10
2. What are the first three ordinal numbers? 10	7. What two seasons interrupt Ordinary Time in the spring? 10
3. What is the longest season in the Church year? 10	8. What do we celebrate on the last Sunday of Ordinary Time? 10
4. Why is it called **Ordinary Time**? 10	9. What is the liturgical color of Ordinary Time? 10
5. After what season does Ordinary Time begin? 10	10. What does the liturgical color green symbolize? 10

10. **Ordinary Time** Answer Sheet

1. One, two, three, which are our counting numbers

2. First, second, third. Ordinal numbers show the order or rank of things.

3. Ordinary Time, like ordinal numbers

4. The Sundays are numbered in order—not because it is boring

5. The Christmas season

6. Thirty-three or thirty-four

7. Lent and Easter

8. Solemnity of Christ the King

9. Green

10. Hope, growth, and life

Our Lunar Calendar

By observing the evening sky, ancient peoples noticed that the moon moved through a cycle lasting twenty-eight to thirty nights. Each night the shape of the moon was slightly different from the previous night. It developed from a new moon to a full moon and back again to a new moon. These ancestors created the lunar calendar, based on the cycles of the moon.

Using the lunar cycle as the basis for calculating the passage of time posed a difficulty, however, since the lunar year is only 354 days long. This is eleven days shorter than the solar cycle. Within only a few years any lunar calendar was no longer aligned with the constellations of the night and the seasons of the year.

The Hebrew people used a lunar calendar borrowed from their Babylonian neighbors. Their celebration of the Passover began each year on the evening of the 14th of Nissan on the lunar calendar. Since the date of the Passover was also determined by the vernal equinox, an extra month was added to the Hebrew calendar every few years to keep the calendar in time with the seasons.

The Romans, from whom we have taken our current calendar, began with a lunar calendar. Since this method of determining the months required constant updating, in the year 46 BCE* the Emperor Julius Caesar decreed the use of a solar calendar. With small revisions made along the way, the Julian calendar was used in Europe until the sixteenth century. In 1582 CE,* Pope Gregory XIII permanently aligned the date of Easter with the vernal equinox by refining the occurrence of leap years.

A blend of both the solar and lunar calendars, this new Gregorian calendar was not accepted in England and the United States until 1752. As years passed, other countries eventually accepted this revised calendar as their commercial and civil calendar. Many other calendars are used in our world today, especially for religious or traditional cultural celebrations.

Find out more about lunar calendars on the Internet or at the library. You can gather information about the Julian calendar, Gregorian calendar, Gregory XIII, lunar calendar, Chinese calendar, Jewish calendar, and lunar phases.

---

*CE stands for the Common Era. It is often used instead of AD (an abbreviation for *anno Domini* or the year of the Lord), to respect the multitude of religious traditions in our world today. BCE (Before the Common Era) replaces BC (Before Christ).

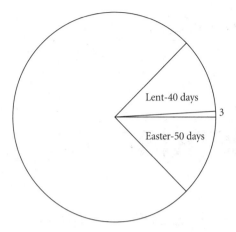

Moveable Feasts

The center of our life as Christians is the Paschal mystery, the suffering, death, and resurrection of Jesus Christ. The center of our liturgical calendar is the celebration of that mystery at Easter. During the Council of Nicea in 325, all the Christian churches agreed that the celebration of the Christian pasch would take place on the Sunday following the first full moon after the vernal equinox. Because this feast is determined by a lunar occurrence, the date of Easter changes each year. So the days we observe in connection with Easter are called "moveable feasts."

Our lenten preparation for the Easter Triduum lasts forty days, from Ash Wednesday to the eve of Holy Thursday. During these days we who are already baptized prepare for the renewal of our baptism at the Easter Vigil. We are privileged to travel with those preparing to be baptized and we make Lent a time of prayer, fasting, and almsgiving.

Each year before our Catholic ancestors began their lenten observances, they kept a season of feasting and merrymaking. This Carnival season began after Twelfth Night and ended with Mardi Gras, the day before Ash Wednesday. During those days, people used up their meat and dairy products, which could not be eaten during the lenten fast. Hence, the word "Carnival" comes from the Latin words *carne* (meat) and *vale* (farewell), meaning "farewell to meat."

In the days immediately before Lent, people confessed their sins and received absolution. They were shriven, or absolved, from their sins. They performed penance for their sins during Lent. The days when they confessed and were absolved from their sins became known as Shrovetide.

The Easter season lasts for fifty days until the celebration of Pentecost. This time of mystagogy, or "unfolding the mysteries," gives us a chance to reflect more deeply on the meaning of the Easter sacraments. Moveable feasts continue until the feasts of the Sacred Heart and Immaculate Heart of Mary, almost three weeks later.

Good topics for library and Internet research include moveable feasts, carnival, Mardi Gras, Lent, Pentecost, Easter, Triduum, and Corpus Christi Procession.

Lunar Games

For an overview of the moveable feasts, begin with the Lunar Calendar game. The rest of the games in this set can be used to prepare for the observance of Lent, the Triduum, and the Easter season.

Carnival: before Ash Wednesday
Lent and Conversion: early in the forty days
Initiation: any time you have participants in RCIA
Triduum: at the end of Lent, the holiest days of the Church year
Easter: before or after Easter
Shepherd: before the fourth Sunday of Easter
Pentecost: during the sixth week of Easter
Corpus Christi: right after Pentecost

Families can enjoy some of these activities during the school spring break. When the date of Easter falls late in April, the last few games can be done on the given feasts during summer vacation.

Before beginning this set of games read *Companion to the Calendar*, pages 11 to 24. There is also great information about some of the terms contained in each game in *A Child's First Catholic Dictionary*.

Lunar: Ash Wednesday, Easter, Lent, Church Year, Pentecost, resurrection

Carnival: absolution, Ash Wednesday, Baptism of Jesus, Easter, Lent, liturgical colors, Palm Sunday, penance, sin

Lent: Alleluia, Easter, fast, Lent, liturgical colors, pilgrimage, prayer, Stations of the Cross

Conversion: conversion, fasting, penance, alms, prayer, reconciliation, sin, works of mercy

Initiation: Baptism, Confirmation, Easter, Eucharist, gospels, Lent, sign of the cross, Word

Triduum: Baptism, creed, Easter, Eucharist, evil, Good Friday, Holy Thursday, Holy Week, Last Supper, Lord's Supper, Paschal Mystery, mystery, Satan, sin

Easter: apostles, ascension, bread, death, disciple, Easter, Eucharist, liturgical colors, Lord's Day, Pentecost, resurrection, tomb, witness

Shepherd: bishop, diocese, Good Shepherd, parish, pastor, pope, psalm, Rome, Vatican

Pentecost: apostles, Bible, disciple, dove, Holy Spirit, liturgical colors, Mary, Pentecost

Corpus Christi: body of Christ, bread, consecration, Last Supper, Liturgy of the Eucharist, Mass, Pentecost, unleavened bread, wine

11. **Lunar Calendar** Question Cards

1. What does the word **lunar** mean?

   11

2. What do we call the eve or evening on which the celebration of a feast begins?

   11

3. What is the great vigil of the Sunday after the first full moon in spring?

   11

4. What do we call the three days of celebration of the death and resurrection of Jesus?

   11

5. What do we call the forty days during which we prepare for Easter?

   11

6. What is the first day of our lenten journey?

   11

7. For how many days do we celebrate Easter?

   11

8. What is the last day of the Easter season?

   11

9. Why is Easter called a moveable feast?

   11

10. What season follows the Easter season?

   11

11. **Lunar Calendar** Answer Sheet

1. Moon—of the moon or measured by the moon and its phases

2. Vigil

3. Easter Vigil

4. Triduum

5. Lent

6. Ash Wednesday

7. Fifty days

8. Pentecost

9. It comes on a different **date** each year depending on how soon the full moon arrives after the spring equinox

10. Ordinary Time, which began after the Christmas season and stopped at Ash Wednesday, now continues until Advent

12. **Carnival** Question Cards

1. What church season do we observe between the Baptism of the Lord and the beginning of Lent?

    12

2. What is the liturgical color for Ordinary Time?

    12

3. What is the name for the day before Lent begins?

    12

4. What does the word **carnival** mean?

    12

5. In medieval times, what foods needed to be consumed before the period of abstinence during Lent?

    12

6. What were the three days before Lent called in medieval times?

    12

7. On what day does Lent begin?

    12

8. What do we receive on our forehead on Ash Wednesday?

    12

9. What is used to make the ashes?

    12

10. What is the meaning of wearing ashes?

    12

12. **Carnival** Answer Sheet

1. Ordinary Time

2. Green, which signifies hope and growth

3. Mardi Gras, which is French for Fat, or Greasy, Tuesday

4. Farewell to meat; it is a season of merrymaking before the lenten abstinence from meat

5. Meat and meat by-products such as eggs, cheese, butter, and lard, which were not eaten during Lent

6. Shrovetide, a time for confession and receiving absolution which was called being shriven. During Lent people lived out the penance given to them in confession.

7. Ash Wednesday

8. Ashes, in the shape of a cross

9. The palms from Passion/Palm Sunday the previous year

10. Grief, repentance

13. **Lent** Question Cards

1. What is the season of preparation for Easter?

13

2. How long does Lent last?

13

3. What is the biblical meaning of the number forty?

13

4. What is the liturgical color for Lent?

13

5. What word is not used in the liturgy during Lent?

13

6. What is a pilgrimage?

13

7. What pilgrimage is made in our own church buildings?

13

8. How many Stations of the Cross are there?

13

9. What are Christians preparing for during Lent?

13

10. What does the white garment of the newly baptized symbolize? (Galatians 3:27)

13

13. **Lent** Answer Sheet

1. Lent (CCC #1438)

2. Forty days; this is not an exact number but a symbolic number

3. Trial, testing, or waiting

4. Violet

5. Alleluia

6. A journey undertaken for religious reasons

7. The Stations of the Cross

8. Fourteen; Pope Paul VI added a fifteenth station, "The Resurrection."

9. To renew our baptism

10. The person has "put on Christ."

14. **Conversion** Question Cards

1. What is sin? 14	6. What is prayer? 14
2. What is the meaning of the word **conversion**? 14	7. In whose name should we offer our prayers? 14
3. Which sacrament celebrates our renewed conversion? 14	8. What can we abstain from other than meat? 14
4. What is a penance? 14	9. What are alms? 14
5. What are the three traditional practices of Lent? 14	10. What do we call the charitable actions by which we help others? 14

14. **Conversion** Answer Sheet

1. An offense against or failure to love God and our neighbor
   (CCC #1849, #1850)

2. Turning one's life around, away from sin and back to Christ
   (CCC #1427)

3. The sacrament of penance or reconciliation

4. An action to help us make up for the harm done by our sin
   (CCC #1459)

5. Prayer, fasting, and almsgiving; since Vatican II, study of our faith
   and of the word of God is also stressed (CCC #1434)

6. Raising one's mind and heart to God (CCC #2559)

7. Jesus (John 14:13)

8. Sinful thoughts, words, and actions

9. Money given to the poor

10. Works of mercy

15. **Initiation** Question Cards

1. Unbaptized adults prepare for the sacraments of initiation through what process?

   15

2. What is the person called who asks about becoming a follower of Christ?

   15

3. What are inquirers marked with when they are welcomed into the catechumenate?

   15

4. What are inquirers called once they are accepted into the catechumenate?

   15

5. What do catechumens hear and learn to follow?

   15

6. What oil is used to anoint and strengthen those preparing for baptism?

   15

7. What do we call the baptized person who accompanies a catechumen on this journey?

   15

8. When is the final intense period of accepting the gospel of Jesus Christ and renouncing sin?

   15

9. When do the elect celebrate the sacraments of initiation?

   15

10. What are the three sacraments of initiation?

    15

15. **Initiation** Answer Sheet

1. The Rite of Christian Initiation of Adults, or RCIA (CCC #1229)

2. An inquirer

3. The Sign of the Cross (CCC #1235)

4. Catechumens (CCC #1247)

5. The word of God (CCC #1236)

6. The oil of catechumens (CCC #1237)

7. A sponsor

8. During Lent; it is called the period of Purification and Enlightenment

9. At the Easter Vigil celebration

10. Baptism, confirmation, and Eucharist

16. **Triduum** Question Cards

1. When does Lent end? 16	6. On which day do we remember how Jesus died for us? 16
2. What is the Triduum? 16	7. What do we light at the beginning of the Easter Vigil? 16
3. What is the paschal mystery we celebrate during the Triduum? 16	8. What do we reject in the baptismal promises? 16
4. What two events do we remember at the Mass of the Lord's Supper on Holy Thursday? 16	9. What words are used when a person is baptized? 16
5. What commandment did Jesus give us at the Last Supper? (John 15:13) 16	10. What prayer do we say after the homily each Sunday to profess our faith? 16

16. **Triduum** Answer Sheet

1. At sunset on Holy Thursday

2. The "three days," from sunset on Holy Thursday until sunset on Easter Sunday

3. The suffering, death, and resurrection of Jesus Christ

4. The washing of feet and the gift of the Eucharist

5. "Love one another as I have loved you."

6. Good Friday

7. New fire and then of the Paschal candle

8. Sin, evil, and Satan

9. "I baptize you in the name of the Father and of the Son and of the Holy Spirit."

10. The Creed, the Profession of Faith: "We believe in one God, the Father…"

17. **Easter** Question Cards

1. What do we celebrate on Easter Sunday?

   (Matthew 28:5–6, Mark 16:6–7, Luke 24:1–5, John 20:11–17)

   17

2. Who told the apostles about the resurrection of Jesus?

   17

3. How many days did Jesus remain on earth before he ascended into heaven?

   (Acts 1:3)

   17

4. How did the disciples on the road to Emmaus recognize Jesus? (Luke 24:30–31)

   17

5. On which day each week do Christians gather to break bread?

   17

6. What is the source and summit of our Christian life?

   17

7. Which Sunday is the center of the entire Church or liturgical year?

   17

8. How do we determine what date to celebrate Easter?

   17

9. What is the liturgical color for Easter?

   17

10. How long does the Easter season last?

    17

17. **Easter** Answer Sheet

1. Jesus' resurrection from the dead (CCC #2174)

2. Mary Magdalene and the holy women who had gone to the tomb (CCC #641)

3. Forty days (CCC #659)

4. In the breaking of the bread (CCC #1329)

5. Sunday, the Lord's Day, the first day of the week

6. The Eucharist (CCC #1324)

7. Easter (CCC #1169)

8. It is the first Sunday after the first full moon following the vernal or spring equinox (CCC #1170)

9. White, sometimes gold

10. Fifty days, until Pentecost

18. **Shepherd** Question Cards

1. On which Sunday are the Scripture readings about shepherds? 18	6. Who shepherds all the faith communities in a diocese? 18
2. What is the first verse of the twenty-third psalm? 18	7. What is the shepherd's staff that the bishop carries in formal ceremonies? 18
3. What is the shepherd's job? 18	8. What are the three jobs of the bishop in leading the faith communities? 18
4. Who is the leader of a parish? 18	9. What name do we usually call the bishop of Rome? 18
5. What is the name of the pastor of your parish? 18	10. What do we call bishops who wear red and elect the pope? 18

18. **Shepherd** Answer Sheet

1. Good Shepherd Sunday or the Fourth Sunday of Easter

2. "The Lord is my shepherd; nothing shall I want."

3. To care for the sheep

4. Pastor, from the Latin word **pastore**, meaning shepherd (CCC #1551)

5. Answer is specific to your parish (CCC #2179)

6. The bishop (CCC #1560)

7. A crosier

8. To teach, sanctify, and guide (CCC #939)

9. The Pope (CCC #882)

10. The cardinals

19. **Pentecost** Question Cards

1. What is the last day of the Easter season?

   19

2. What does the word **Pentecost** mean?

   19

3. What is the liturgical color for Pentecost?

   19

4. Before Jesus ascended into heaven, whom did he promise to send?

   (John 16:5–7, Luke 24:49)

   19

5. In which book of the Bible do we find the story of Pentecost?

   19

6. Who waited together in prayer in the upper room?

   (Acts 1:13–14)

   19

7. What noise was heard on Pentecost? (Acts 2:2)

   19

8. What appeared over the head of each person in the upper room? (Acts 2:3)

   19

9. What were the disciples able to do after they received the Spirit? (Acts 2:4)

   19

10. What did the people hear the disciples speaking about?

   (Acts 2:11)

   19

19. **Pentecost** Answer Sheet

1. Pentecost Sunday

2. Fiftieth day

3. Red

4. The Holy Spirit (CCC #729)

5. Acts of the Apostles

6. The apostles, the women in their company, Mary the mother of Jesus, and his relatives

7. A noise like a strong driving wind

8. Divided tongues as of fire (CCC #696)

9. Speak in other languages

10. The mighty things God had done

20. **Corpus Christi** Question Cards

1. What do we call the second Sunday after Pentecost on which we honor the Eucharist?

   20

2. When did Jesus leave us his body and blood in the Eucharist?

   20

3. What do we present at the preparation of the gifts at Mass?

   20

4. What does the word **Eucharist** mean?

   20

5. What is our response to "Let us proclaim the mystery of faith"?

   20

6. What word do we say at the end of the Eucharistic Prayer to proclaim: "Yes, we believe"?

   20

7. How did the disciples at Emmaus recognize Jesus?

   20

8. What are the two meanings of "Body of Christ"?

   20

9. At the end of Mass what are we are sent forth to do?

   20

10. In what ways is Christ present in our celebration of the Eucharist?

   20

20. **Corpus Christi** Answer Sheet

1. The Body and Blood of Christ, formerly called Corpus Christi; the celebration often included an outdoor eucharistic procession

2. At the Last Supper (CCC #1322)

3. Bread and wine; gifts for the poor can also be presented (CCC #1350–1351)

4. Thanksgiving (CCC #1328)

5. The usual response: Christ has died! Christ is risen! Christ will come again! (There are also three other options.) (CCC #1354)

6. Amen

7. In the breaking of the bread (CCC #1329)

8. The Eucharist and the Church (CCC #789, #1333)

9. To love and serve our God; the word "Mass" comes from the Latin word **missa**, meaning to mission or to send forth (CCC #1332)

10. In the Eucharist shared, the word proclaimed, the priest presiding, and in the assembly gathered (CCC #1088)

Our Catholic Environment

As Christians, we surround ourselves with symbols of our faith. In this way our senses become a vehicle to remind us of the truths we hold dear. In our churches, as well as in our homes, we use art and devotions that help us raise our minds and hearts to God. In addition, we find signs of God in creation.

Learning proper liturgical terms for vessels, vestments, and architecture can lead to a deeper understanding of our worship space. Checking out some resource books or searching on the Internet will help as well. For example, look up liturgical vestments, church architecture, and altar vessels.

Two wonderful books to read before or after these games are *A Walk through Our Church* and *A Peek into My Church*. With *A Child's First Catholic Dictionary* spend some time reading about the terms that connect with the various sets of questions.

Sanctuary: altar, body of Christ, ciborium, cross, crucifix, gospels, host, mass, tabernacle

Altar: altar, chalice, ciborium, consecration, Eucharist, mass, server, water, wine

Baptistry: Baptism, Baptism of Jesus, baptismal font, chrism, godparents, holy water, water

Vestments: alb, chasuble, deacon, liturgical colors, priest, stole, vestments

Lectionary: Bible, Church Year, evangelists, gospel, lectionary, lector, Liturgy of the Word

Devotions: Advent, Christmas, cross, crucifix, incense, nativity, rosary, sacramental, Stations of the Cross

Prayer gestures: genuflect, gospel, sign of peace, prayer, Sign of the Cross

Cross: cross, crucifix, death, Good Friday, Jesus, passion

Church: baptismal font, bishop, Body of Christ, chapel, church, saints

Creation: creation, Creator, temptation

21. **Sanctuary** Question Cards

1. What is the large table used for the celebration of the Eucharist?

    21

2. What is the stand from which the reader proclaims the word of God?

    21

3. What do we call the chair set aside for the leader of our worship?

    21

4. What do we call the area of the church that contains the altar, ambo, and presider's chair?

    21

5. What do we call a cross with an image of Jesus on it?

    21

6. What is the decorated book containing the readings about the life of Jesus?

    21

7. What small side table holds the vessels used at Mass?

    21

8. What is the covered cup that holds the extra hosts after communion?

    21

9. What is the cabinet in which the church reserves the Eucharist to bring to the sick?

    21

10. What lamp left burning near the tabernacle shows that the Blessed Sacrament is present?

    21

21. **Sanctuary** Answer Sheet

1. Altar (CCC #1182, #1383)

2. Lectern or ambo (CCC #1184)

3. Presider's chair (CCC #1184)

4. Sanctuary

5. A crucifix

6. **Book of the Gospels**

7. Credence table

8. Ciborium

9. Tabernacle (CCC #1183, #1379)

10. Sanctuary lamp

22. **Altar Setting** Question Cards

1. What is the fabric covering placed on the table on which the eucharistic sacrifice is offered?

   22

2. What is the large book used by the presider, containing the prayers used at Mass?

   22

3. What is the square linen cloth, like a place mat, that is placed on the center of the altar?

   22

4. What is the plate on which we place the altar bread?

   22

5. What is the stemmed cup used to hold the wine?

   22

6. What are the pieces of folded linen used by the Eucharistic ministers to wipe the rim of the cup after each person drinks?

   22

7. What are the small pitchers that hold the wine and water at Mass?

   22

8. What are the hosts?

   22

9. What is placed on the altar and lit as a sign of reverence and festivity?

   22

10. What is the small metal box with a hinged cover used to carry communion to someone who is sick?

   22

22. **Altar Setting** Answer Sheet

1. Altar cloth

2. **Sacramentary** or **Roman Missal**

3. Corporal

4. Paten

5. Chalice

6. Purificators

7. Cruets

8. The altar bread consecrated at Mass

9. Candles

10. Pyx

23. **Baptistry** Question Cards

1. What is the large container for water used at baptism?

   23

2. What is the large candle on a tall stand blessed and lit during the Easter Vigil?

   23

3. What is the special area of the church containing the baptismal font and used for baptisms?

   23

4. What are the small bowls by the doors of the church that are filled with holy water we use to bless ourselves?

   23

5. What small cupboard holds the blessed oils?

   23

6. Which oil is used to anoint the newly baptized?

   23

7. What do the newly baptized receive with the words "Receive the light of Christ"?

   23

8. What does the baptismal garment symbolize?

   23

9. What color is the baptismal garment?

   23

10. What white cloth, reminding us of our baptism, is placed on the casket at the beginning of a funeral?

   23

23. **Baptistry** Answer Sheet

1. Baptismal font or pool

2. Paschal Candle (CCC #1243)

3. Baptistry (CCC #1185)

4. Holy water font (CCC #1185)

5. Ambry (CCC #1183)

6. Chrism (CCC #1241)

7. A baptismal candle lit from the Paschal Candle

8. That the person has "put on Christ" (CCC #1243)

9. White (CCC #1243)

10. A pall

24. **Vestments** Question Cards

1. What are vestments?

24

2. What long white tunic do the ministers wear at worship?

24

3. What do we call a cord used as a belt over the alb?

24

4. What do we call the long scarf-like cloth worn over the shoulders of an ordained minister?

24

5. Which ordained ministers wear the stole over only one shoulder and to the side?

24

6. What is the stole a sign of?

24

7. What colored outer garment is worn by a priest presiding at Mass?

24

8. What are the different colors of the liturgical seasons or feasts?

24

9. What is the special hat worn by a bishop on formal occasions?

24

10. What is the staff with a crook or cross on top that a bishop carries in his hand?

24

24. **Vestments** Answer Sheet

1. Special garments worn by ministers during the liturgy; some vestments are worn only by ordained ministers

2. The alb, which reminds us of our baptismal garment

3. Cincture

4. Stole

5. Deacons

6. A person's ordination

7. Chasuble

8. Violet for Lent and Advent, green for Ordinary Time, white for joyous feasts of Our Lord and the saints, red for Pentecost and martyrs

9. Miter

10. Crosier

25. **Lectionary** Question Cards

1. Which book contains the Bible passages proclaimed at the liturgy? 25	6. Which gospel is proclaimed on Sundays in Cycle B? 25
2. How many years or cycles of readings are there in the Sunday lectionary? 25	7. Which gospel is proclaimed on Sundays in Cycle C? 25
3. What does the word **gospel** mean? 25	8. During which season each year is the gospel of John proclaimed? 25
4. What are the four gospels in the Christian Scripture? 25	9. When does the liturgical or Church year begin? 25
5. Which gospel is proclaimed on Sundays in Cycle A? 25	10. Which cycle of readings do we read from this year? 25

25. **Lectionary** Answer Sheet

1. Lectionary

2. Three, called Cycles A, B, and C

3. Good news

4. Matthew, Mark, Luke, and John

5. Matthew

6. Mark

7. Luke

8. The Easter season

9. The First Sunday of Advent or the fourth Sunday before Christmas

10. Answer depends on the current year. Any year that is evenly divisible by three is Cycle C. From this you can determine the present year. (Example: 2010 ÷ 3 = 668 with no remainder, so it is Cycle C.)

26. **Devotions** Question Cards

1. What do we call an image that is carved or cast to represent Jesus or one of the saints?

26

2. What are the pictures on the walls of a church that show Jesus on the way to his death?

26

3. What do we call the small candles in glass holders that we light for a special intention?

26

4. What is the perfumed smoke used in church, that rises with our prayers?

26

5. What is the sun-burst shaped container used during Benediction so we can see the host?

26

6. What string of beads do we use in praying to Mary?

26

7. What is a cross with an image of Christ on it?

26

8. What is the ring of greens containing four candles that we light during the weeks before Christmas?

26

9. What do we call a set of objects representing the story of the birth of Jesus?

26

10. What is the candle lit by the bride and groom together at their wedding?

26

26. **Devotions** Answer Sheet

1. Statue (CCC #1161)

2. Stations of the Cross

3. Vigil lights or votive candles

4. Incense

5. Monstrance

6. Rosary (CCC #2678)

7. Crucifix

8. Advent wreath

9. Nativity set or Christmas crèche

10. Unity candle

27. **Prayer Gestures** Question Cards

1. What prayer gesture do we use at the beginning of Mass to show we belong to Jesus?

   27

2. How do we show respect for the word of God read during the liturgy?

   27

3. How do we sign ourselves before the reading of the gospel?

   27

4. During which Scripture reading do we stand to show special respect?

   27

5. How do we extend the peace of Christ during Mass?

   27

6. In what position are the presider's hands when he offers prayers?

   27

7. What are the three processions during the Sunday liturgy?

   27

8. How does the presider honor the **Book of the Gospels** after reading the gospel?

   27

9. How do we hold our hands to receive communion in them?

   27

10. With what action do we honor the Eucharistic Christ in the tabernacle?

   27

27. **Prayer Gestures** Answer Sheet

1.   The sign of the cross

2.   We sit quietly, give our full attention, and concentrate

3.   On our forehead, lips, and over our heart to show our desire for the gospel to be in our minds, on our lips, and in our hearts

4.   The gospel

5.   A kiss, an embrace, a handshake

6.   He holds them outward, in the orans position

7.   Entrance, preparation of the gifts, and communion

8.   By kissing it

9.   Extend the left hand supported by the right hand—"Make a throne of your hands to receive the King" (Cyril of Jerusalem)

10. A genuflection or a deep bow

28. **The Cross in Art** Question Cards

1. On what did Jesus die? <div style="text-align:right">28</div>	6. What does **INRI** stand for? (John 19:19) <div style="text-align:right">28</div>
2. What boating symbol was used as a hidden cross for early persecuted Christians? <div style="text-align:right">28</div>	7. What does a Greek cross look like? <div style="text-align:right">28</div>
3. What did medieval Christian artists put on the cross to show the glory of the resurrection? <div style="text-align:right">28</div>	8. What is a tau cross shaped like? <div style="text-align:right">28</div>
4. What do we call a cross with an image of Jesus on it? <div style="text-align:right">28</div>	9. What does a Celtic cross have where the bars intersect? <div style="text-align:right">28</div>
5. On a Latin cross which beam is longer? <div style="text-align:right">28</div>	10. What do we call the cross that is carried in at the beginning of Mass? <div style="text-align:right">28</div>

28. **The Cross in Art** Answer Sheet

1. A cross

2. The anchor—the top part of an anchor is in the shape of a cross

3. Jewels or precious stones

4. A crucifix

5. The upright or vertical beam

6. **Iesus Nazarenus Rex Iudaeorum**—Latin for "Jesus of Nazareth, King of the Jews," the inscription Pilate had posted on the cross of Jesus

7. The beams are of equal length, like the cross used by the Red Cross organization

8. Like the Greek letter tau (T), with the cross beam on top of the vertical beam

9. A circle

10. A processional cross

29. **Church** Question Cards

1. What do we call a Christian house of prayer where people assemble to celebrate the Eucharist?

   29

2. What do we call the Body of Christ or the faithful community of believers?

   29

3. Why do we have a vestibule leading into the church?

   29

4. Why do you think the baptismal font is often placed by the entrance to the church?

   29

5. What do we call the large area of a church building where people sit?

   29

6. What do we call the area of the church that contains the altar, ambo, and presider's chair?

   29

7. What do we call the colored windows showing a scene or design?

   29

8. Where are the vessels and vestments kept when not in use?

   29

9. What special name is given to the bishop's church?

   29

10. What is the meaning of the twelve candle sconces and crosses when found on the walls around the nave of a church?

    29

29. **Church** Answer Sheet

1. A church (CCC #1181)

2. The Church (CCC #752)

3. This space helps us make the transition from the outside world into the church (CCC #1186)

4. We enter the Church (people of God) through baptism and we enter the church building through the door past the font

5. Nave—this word is used because years ago the Church (people of God) was compared to a ship sailing on its journey toward eternal life (CCC #845)

6. Sanctuary

7. Stained glass windows

8. Sacristy

9. A cathedral, named for the bishop's chair (**cathedra**) which is in the sanctuary of the cathedral (CCC #1184)

10. The church building has been consecrated or solemnly set aside as a permanent worship space

30. **God's Creation** Question Cards

1. What did God create? 30	6. Who is the patron saint of ecology? 30
2. What does creation give us a glimpse of? 30	7. What do we call making used materials into new items? 30
3. Who shares responsibility for caring for the earth? 30	8. Which country wastes the most of earth's goods? 30
4. With whom do we need to share the goods of creation? 30	9. What do we call the desire to do something we know we should avoid? 30
5. What is the study of the relationship between living things and the environment? 30	10. What virtue helps us balance our desire for material goods? 30

30. **God's Creation** Answer Sheet

1. The world and everything in it (CCC #279)

2. The beauty and greatness of God (CCC #1147, #339)

3. Each one of us (CCC #307)—"care for God's creation" is one of the principles of Catholic social teaching

4. All people, including generations to come (CCC #2415)

5. Ecology

6. Francis of Assisi (CCC #2416)

7. Recycling

8. The United States

9. Temptation (CCC #1707)

10. Temperance

Recommended Resources

Catechism of the Catholic Church (United States Catholic Conference, 1997)

The Catholic Source Book by Rev. Peter Klein (Harcourt Religion Publishers, 2007)

A Child's First Catholic Dictionary by Richard Dyches, Thomas Mustachio, Ansgar Holmberg (Ave Maria Press, 1994)

Companion to the Calendar: A Guide to the Saints and Mysteries of the Christian Calendar by Mary Ellen Hynes (Liturgy Training Publications, 1994)

To Dance with God: Family Ritual and Community Celebration by Gertrud Mueller Nelson (Paulist Press, 1986)

A Peek into My Church by Wendy Goody, Veronica Kelly, Ginny Pruitt (Whippersnapper, 1999)

Pocket Catholic Dictionary by John Hardon (Image Books, 1985)

The Story of Clocks and Calendars by Betsy Maestro, Giulio Maestro (Lothrop, Lee, and Shepard, 1999)

A Walk through Our Church by Gertrud Mueller Nelson (Paulist Press, 1998)